P9-DCZ-909

MACMILLAN/McGRAW-HILL

Math

Exploration Activity Guide

Grade 4

Macmillan McGraw-Hill

The **McGraw·Hill** Companies

Macmillan McGraw-Hill

Published by Macmillan/McGraw-Hill, of McGraw-Hill Education, a division of The McGraw-Hill Companies, Inc., Two Penn Plaza, New York, New York 10121.

Copyright © by Macmillan/McGraw-Hill. All rights reserved. No part of this publication may be reproduced or distributed in any form or by any means, or stored in a database or retrieval system, without the prior written consent of The McGraw-Hill Companies, Inc., including, but not limited to, network storage or transmission, or broadcast for distance learning.

Printed in the United States of America

5 6 7 8 9 073 08 07 06 05

Contents

Purpose of This Book

Macmillan/McGraw-Hill's *Exploration Activity Guide* provides teachers with an opportunity to choose an alternate hands-on method of presenting the mathematical concepts for selected lessons within each chapter of *Macmillan/McGraw-Hill Math.*

Each page in the guide provides a supplemental activity that develops mathematical concepts by allowing students to actively build new knowledge from prior knowledge and experience.

© Macmillan/McGraw-Hill

How To Use This Book

Each page of this *Exploration Activity Guide* provides a hands-on activity to supplement the concept developed within the identified lesson from *Macmillan/McGraw-Hill Math.*

Each activity title is followed by an identifier indicating which lesson from the chapter this activity supplements. The *What You Will Explore* section gives an overview of the activity and *Materials* gives a list of materials needed.

A description of the activity is contained in the *Task* box. In *What to Look For and What to Ask* suggested questions are provided for the teacher to help guide students to the understanding of the lesson concept. *Share and Discuss* questions are provided to stimulate class discussion. The *Key Idea* section identifies the key mathematical concept this activity develops. *Follow-Up* provides an idea of how to extend the activity.

Examples of student work are provided for each activity.

© Macmillan/McGraw-Hill

Estimate Quantities

Alternate activities for **Teach** *in Lesson 1.1.*

The Task

Ask students if they remember using bean sticks when they were in Grade 1. Explain that they are going to make bean sticks for Grade 1.

■ **You need to estimate how many beans are in your container so you can figure out about how many sticks are needed. About how many beans are in your container?**

▶ **What You Will Explore**

Students investigate estimation. They decide on quantities that are easy to visualize and to use as benchmark numbers. They use these benchmarks to help determine the quantity in the total collection.

Materials
(per student pair)
• about 100 beans or small items in a clear plastic container
• grid paper and crayons

What to Look For and What to Ask

As students work, check to see that they have first created a reasonable benchmark, and then used it to estimate the total.

Ask students to retell the problem in their own words.

• **When you estimate will you know exactly how many there are in the container?**

• **Is it important to know exactly how many beans are in your container? Why or why not?**

• **How can you use a smaller number of beans to estimate how many there are in the container?**

• **What do you think a benchmark number is?**

Share and Discuss

Ask students to share their strategies for determining how many beans are in their containers. For example, as Ellie shows in her work, she circled 10 beans on the paper. She then spread the rest of the beans on the same paper and circled groups of about 10 beans.

Ask students questions along the way:

• **How did you use the benchmark number?**

• **How did the benchmark number help you estimate the number of beans in the container?**

Key Idea As students share their answers, point out that the benchmark number is always a smaller number that you can count easily.

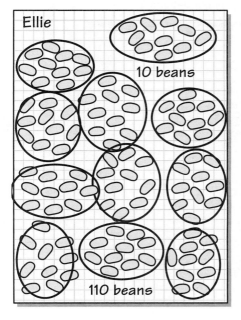

Ellie
10 beans
110 beans

Follow-Up Activity

Have students figure out a way to find out how close their estimates were.

▶ **What You Will Explore**

Students investigate how to find the difference or change between the amount of money given and the cost of a purchase. Students use coins and develop strategies to count up from the cost of a purchase to the dollar amount given for payment.

Materials

(per student pair)
• dollar bills and coins (play money from Teaching Tools)
• paper and pencils

Count Up to Find the Change

Alternate activities for **Teach** *in Lesson 2.1.*

The Task

Ask students to pretend that they are store clerks.

■ **There is an assortment of bills and coins in the cashier's drawer at the Green Market. How much would you give in change if a customer bought something that cost $8.39 and paid with a $10 bill?**

What to Look For and What to Ask

Observe students as they make change to see that they are using coins and bills that will take them from $8.39 to $10.00.

Ask questions to stimulate discussion.

• **What are some different ways you could use to decide how much change to give?**

• **How can you use counting to figure out which bills and coins to give in change?**

• **When you count your change, would you count the dollar bills or the coins first?**

Share and Discuss

As students share their answers, discuss the strategies they used to find the amount of change to be given to the customer. For example, in the work pictured, Marc used coins to count up from $8.39 to $9 and then counted up $1.00 to $10 to get $1.61 in change. Leanna counted the dollar first and then counted the coins to get $1.61 in change.

You may wish to ask questions such as:

• **How did you count to find the change?**

• **Which bills and coins make the change?**

Key Idea As students share how they found the change, point out that when giving change, you usually give the least number of coins and bills possible.

Follow-Up Activity

The cashier's drawer at the Green Market has the following bills: one $10, two $5, and five $1. It also has the following coins: four quarters, ten dimes, ten nickels, and 53 pennies. What is the total value of the money in the drawer? Show how you counted.

Marc

	(1¢)	(10¢)	(50¢)	($1)	*change = $1.61*
$8.39	$8.40	$8.50	$9	$10	

Leanna

	($1)	(1¢)	(10¢)	(50¢)	*change = $1.61*
$8.39	$9.39	$9.40	$9.50	$10	

▶ **What You Will Explore**

Students investigate adding larger numbers. They use basic addition facts, and powers of 10 to find addition patterns and the sum.

Materials

(per student pair)
- 20 counters or color tiles
- paper and pencils

Use Patterns to Add

Alternate activities for **Teach** *in Lesson 3.3.*

The Task

Ask students to think about how they would solve the following problem.

■ **Some airlines give points for using the airline. Travelers can use these points for free travel. To travel from Los Angeles to New York City and back might take 30,000 points. To go from New York City to London and back takes another 60,000 points. How many points would it take to go from Los Angeles to New York to London and back?**

What to Look For and What to Ask

Observe students to make sure that they understand the task and are taking appropriate steps to complete it.

Ask students to retell the problem in their own words.

- **What operation can you use to find out how many points it will take?**
- **How can you use addition facts to help you?**
- **How can you use an addition pattern to help you find the total?**
- **How can you use number sentences to show the pattern and the total?**

Share and Discuss

After students have finished adding the points, ask them to share their addition patterns and to tell about the strategies they used for finding the total. For example, in the work pictured, Jeff began with the addition facts and then used a pattern by adding a zero each time to both addends until he reached the amounts in the problem.

Jeff
$3 + 6 = 9$
$30 + 60 = 90$
$300 + 600 = 900$
$3,000 + 6,000 = 9,000$
$30,000 + 60,000 = 90,000$

Ask questions as students share their strategies.

- **What addition facts did you start with?**
- **When each addend has a zero, for example 30 + 60, how many zeros do you add to the sum?**

Key Idea As students share and discuss their answers, point out that addition sentences can be used to show the pattern.

Follow-Up Activity

Have students continue the pattern with 5 zeros in each addend.

Activity 4

▶ **What You Will Explore**

Students investigate subtracting larger numbers. They use basic subtraction facts and powers of 10 to find subtraction patterns and the difference.

Materials
(per student pair)
• paper and pencils

Use Patterns to Subtract

Alternate activities for **Teach** *in Lesson 4.2.*

> ### The Task
>
> Explain to students that sometimes you can use patterns to solve problems.
>
> ■ **About 600,000 people live in Alaska. Hawaii has a population of about 1,200,000. How many more people live in Hawaii than in Alaska?**

What to Look For and What to Ask

Observe students' work to make sure that they understand the task.

Have students retell the problem using their own words.

• **What operation can you use to find out how many more people live in Hawaii?**

• **How can you use subtraction facts to help you?**

• **How can you use a subtraction pattern to help you find the total?**

Share and Discuss

As students share their subtraction patterns, discuss the strategies they used. For example, in the work pictured, Erik used the subtraction facts 12 − 6. He used patterns by adding a zero to each number until the subtraction included the numbers in the problem. Ariel did not use a pattern. She wrote the subtraction fact and then wrote the subtraction problem vertically, aligning the zeros. She circled the 1, 2 and 6 in the vertical subtraction problem and subtracted the numbers.

Take this sharing opportunity by asking questions such as:

• **Did you add or subtract the numbers?**

• **Why did you use the subtraction fact 12 − 6?**

Key Idea As students share their answers and strategies, point out that when using a pattern it is important to add zeros to both numbers. If they don't, they will change the problem.

Follow-Up Activity

Have students continue the pattern by adding another zero to each number.

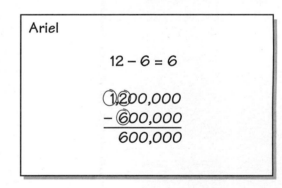

Erik

$12 - 6 = 6$
$120 - 60 = 60$
$1,200 - 600 = 600$
$12,000 - 6,000 = 6,000$
$120,000 - 60,000 = 60,000$
$1,200,000 - 600,000 = 600,000$

Ariel

$12 - 6 = 6$

$$\begin{array}{r} ①②00,000 \\ - ⑥00,000 \\ \hline 600,000 \end{array}$$

Activity

5

▶ **What You Will Explore**

Students investigate and calculate how much time has passed between the beginning and end of a specified time period. They find ways of counting the minutes and hours or converting minutes to hours.

Materials
(per student pair)
• analog clock
• paper and pencils

How Long Does It Take?

Alternate activities for **Teach** *in Lesson 5.2.*

The Task

Tell students the following problem.

■ **The Lacrosse team practices from 3:15 to 5:45 every day. Their Saturday games always begin at 1:30 and are over at 3:15. How long is the practice? How long is the game?**

What to Look For and What to Ask

Observe students as they work to make sure that they understand the task.

Ask students to retell the problem in their own words.

• **When does the team begin their practice?**

• **How can you figure out how long the practice lasts?**

• **When does the Saturday game begin and end?**

• **How can you find out how long the game lasts?**

Share and Discuss

Ask students to share the strategies they used to find out how much time elapsed between the beginning and end of the practice and of the game. For example, in the work pictured, Gina counted on first by the hour and then counted the remaining minutes by 5s. Other students might use their analog clock faces.

Ask questions as students share their strategies.

• **How many minutes are in an hour?**

• **How can you find out how many hours there are in 150 minutes?**

Key Idea As students share and discuss their answers, point out that another name for 15 minutes is a quarter hour, 30 minutes is a half hour, and that one hour is 60 minutes.

Follow-Up Activity

Ask students to compare the time the team spends practicing and the time it spends playing a game. Which lasts longer? How much longer?

Gina

3:15 to 4:15 = 1 hour
4:15 to 5:15 = 1 hour
5:15 → 5:20 → 5:25 → 5:30 → 5:35 → 5:40 → 5:45
   5 min 10 min 15 min 20 min 25 min 30 min
Practice: 2 hours 30 minutes

1:30 to 2:30 = 1 hour
2:30 → 2:35 → 2:40 → 2:45 → 2:50 → 2:55 → 3:00 → 3:05 → 3:10 → 3:15
   5 min 10 min 15 min 20 min 25 min 30 min 35 min 40 min 45 min
Game: 1 hour 45 minutes

Displaying Data in a Bar Graph

Alternate activities for Teach in Lesson 6.2.

> ▶ **What You Will Explore**
>
> Students display collected data in a bar graph. They label the bottom and the side of the graph and give the graph a title.

> **Materials**
> (per student pair)
> - red, white, and blue connecting cubes
> - grid paper; pencils; crayons

The Task

Copy the tally table on the chalkboard and tell students they will use this information.

- **Mr. John's fourth-grade class celebrated Flag Day by wearing red, white, or blue. Make a bar graph using this information. Which color did most students wear?**

Color	Number of Children
Red	卌 卌 l
White	卌 lll
Blue	卌 卌 卌

What to Look For and What to Ask

Observe students' strategies as they work to see that they have chosen a workable method of creating a graph. Ask:

- **Are you going to make a single or double bar graph?**
- **How will you label the bottom and the side of the bar graph?**
- **What will you title the bar graph?**

Share and Discuss

As students share their bar graphs with the class, discuss the strategies they used to create the bar graph, label it, and title it. For example, Edward used grid paper and drew a horizontal bar graph for each color. Other students might use connecting cubes to model the graph first.

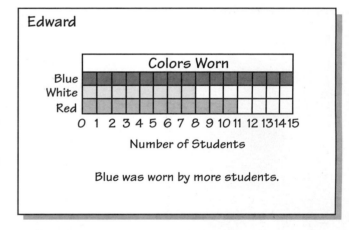

Edward

Colors Worn

Number of Students

Blue was worn by more students.

Ask students questions such as:

- **How do you know how many students wore red, white, or blue?**
- **How can you tell from the graph which color was worn by more students?**

Key Idea As students share their answers and strategies, point out that displaying the information in a bar graph helps to compare data without counting.

Follow-Up Activity

Have students use line plots to display their data.

Order of Factors in Multiplication

Alternate activities for Teach in Lesson 7.2.

▶ **What You Will Explore**

Students investigate properties of multiplication. They make rectangles using color tiles to represent different related facts.

Materials

(per student pair)
- 21 color tiles
- paper and pencils

The Task

Ask students to pretend that they are designing a park bench.

■ **You are going to cover a park bench with tiles. You have 21 tiles to place in the shape of a rectangle. Show two different arrangements and write a multiplication equation for each way. Is there a difference in the product if the order of the factors changes?**

What to Look For and What to Ask

Observe students as they work with the tiles to make sure that they understand the task.

Ask students to retell the problem in their own words.

- **What can you tell about the arrangement?**
- **How can you show it another way?**
- **What do you notice about the two arrangements?**
- **What can you say about the two factors?**

Share and Discuss

Ask students to share their tile arrangements and tell what each set of multiplication equations shows. Discuss with students the strategies they used. For example, in the work pictured, Keri drew the different arrangements and wrote the 4 related facts. Her paper has a written conclusion that the order of the factors does not change the product.

Ask students questions such as:

- **What did you notice about the factors and the product?**
- **What did you notice about the multiplication expression 1 × 21?**

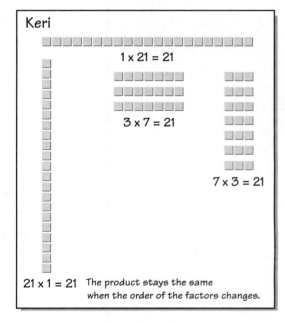

Keri

$1 \times 21 = 21$

$3 \times 7 = 21$

$7 \times 3 = 21$

$21 \times 1 = 21$ The product stays the same when the order of the factors changes.

Key Idea As students share their answers, point out that the order of the factors does not affect the product. This is called the Commutative Property of Multiplication. Then point out that the multiplication of 1 × 21 illustrates the Identity Property of Multiplication.

Follow-Up Activity

Ask students to solve 0 rows with 21 tiles and to identify the multiplication property associated with this multiplication.

▶ What You Will Explore

Students use related multiplication facts to investigate division.

Materials
(per student pair)
- counters
- paper and pencils

Multiply to Divide

Alternate activities for Teach in Lesson 8.2.

The Task

Tell students the following problem.

- **There are 9 classrooms in the Dance Studio. Each classroom has the same number of ceiling lights. There are 72 ceiling lights in all. How many lights are in each classroom?**

What to Look For and What to Ask

Check that students understand the task.

Have students retell the problem in their own words.

- **What operation should you use to find the answer?**
- **How many equal groups of lights do you need?**
- **How can you find the answer using counters?**
- **Can you use a multiplication equation to find the answer?**

Share and Discuss

As students share how they solved the problem, discuss the strategies they used to find the number of lights in each room. For example, in the work pictured, Deanna drew 9 rectangles and put equal groups of counters in each rectangle. Brett showed the division algorithm next to a related multiplication fact.

You may wish to ask questions such as:

- **How are the multiplication and division facts related?**
- **How are multiplication and division related?**

Key Idea As students share their answers, point out that in both multiplication and division you deal with equal groups.

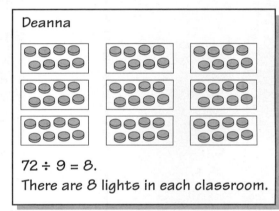

Deanna

$72 \div 9 = 8$.
There are 8 lights in each classroom.

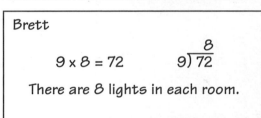

Brett

$9 \times 8 = 72$ $\qquad 9\overline{)72}$ with 8

There are 8 lights in each room.

Follow-Up Activity

Have students solve other problems, such as 7 classrooms with 49 ceiling lights or 54 ceiling lights and 6 classrooms. Ask them to find how many lights in each classroom.

Students investigate the Associative Property of Multiplication and apply patterns when multiplying by powers of ten. They investigate if the order in which three factors are multiplied changes the product.

Materials

(per student pair)
• color tiles
• paper and pencils

Does the Order Matter?

Alternate activities for Teach in Lesson 9.1.

The Task

Ask students to think about how they would solve the following problems.

■ **To celebrate Cliffside's 100th anniversary, students are hanging small flags from the trees outside their schools. They hang 3 flags in each tree. There are 3 trees outside each school and 6 schools in town. How many flags will the students hang?**

■ **There are about 600 trees in the whole town. How many flags would they hang if they hung 3 flags in each tree?**

What to Look For and What to Ask

Observe students' use of their tiles to make sure that they have developed a strategy that will enable them to solve the problems.

Ask students to retell the problem in their own words.

• **How many trees are there outside all the schools in town?**

• **How can you find out how many flags they used?**

• **Will the answer be the same if you multiply the numbers another way?**

• **What kind of pattern can you use to find out how many flags you would need for all the trees in the town?**

Share and Discuss

As they are working, ask students to share their solutions and tell about the strategies they used. For example, in the work pictured, Samantha used color tiles to solve the problem. Below her tiles, she wrote $6 \times 3 \times 3 = 54$. She then showed $3 \times 600 = 1,800$ using a pattern.

Ask students questions such as:

• **Does the order in which you multiply the 3 factors matter?**

• **What is the pattern you used to find out how many flags would be needed for every tree in the town?**

> **Samantha**
>
> $6 \times 3 \times 3 = 54$
>
> They hang 54 flags.
>
> 3×600
>
> $3 \times 6 = 18; 3 \times 60 = 180; 3 \times 600 = 1,800$
>
> They would need 1,800 flags.

Key Idea As students share their equations, point out that when multiplying factors by changing the order of the factors, students apply the Associative Property of Multiplication.

Follow-Up Activity

Have students use different sets of numbers, such as $4 \times 5 \times 2$, and multiply the factors in all possible orders to see that the order of the factors does not change the product.

▶ What You Will Explore

Students investigate multiplying a three-digit number by a one-digit number. They model the multiplication using place-value models. They then record what they showed with the models using a standard multiplication algorithm.

Materials
(per student pair)
• place-value models
• paper and pencils

Use Multiplication and Place-Value Models

Alternate activities for Teach in Lesson 10.1.

The Task

Tell students the following problem.

■ **During a recent Read-a-Thon, the fourth graders pledged to read a certain number of pages. Students kept track of the number of pages they read. Each of 3 students recorded reading a Madison Fin book. Each book had 145 pages. How many pages did the 3 students read?**

What to Look For and What to Ask

Observe students as they use the place-value models to make sure that they understand how to solve the problem.

Have students retell the problem in their own words.

• **How can you find the total number of pages the students read?**

• **How can you use place-value models to show the number of pages the students read?**

• **How can you show what you did with the models using an equation?**

Share and Discuss

As students share how they multiplied, discuss the strategies they used to translate what they did with models into an equation. For example, in the work pictured, Scott used models as well as the multiplication algorithm, showing each step.

You may wish to ask questions such as:

• **In 3 groups of 5 ones, how many tens are there?**

• **How do you show regrouping in multiplication?**

Key Idea As students share their answers, encourage them to tell which operation they used to solve the problem. Remind them that you regroup in multiplication the same way as you regroup in addition.

Follow-Up Activity

Have students use similar numbers, such as 127 pages read by each of 4 students. One partner uses place-value models while the other student writes and solves the corresponding multiplication algorithm.

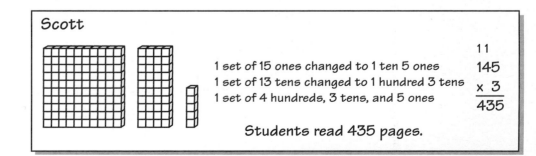

Scott

1 set of 15 ones changed to 1 ten 5 ones
1 set of 13 tens changed to 1 hundred 3 tens
1 set of 4 hundreds, 3 tens, and 5 ones

$$\begin{array}{r} 11 \\ 145 \\ \times\ 3 \\ \hline 435 \end{array}$$

Students read 435 pages.

Students investigate multiplication by the multiples of ten. They use models and the standard algorithm to solve problems.

Materials
(per student pair)
- graph paper
- paper and pencils

Multiply by Tens

Alternate activities for Teach *in Lesson 11.2.*

The Task

Ask students to solve the problem by making models.

- **If you use graph paper and make a model showing 100, you use 10 squares across and 10 squares down.**

- **How can you use graph paper to make a model for 20 × 24?**

What to Look For and What to Ask

Ask students to explain what they are to do. Observe students as they work to see that they are using models to help solve the problem.

- **How many squares across will you draw?**

- **How many squares down will you draw?**

- **When you use these numbers, what shape will you end up with?**

- **How can you use multiplication patterns to find the product of 20 × 24?**

Share and Discuss

Ask students to share how they figured out the total number of squares in the model. Encourage them to show their strategies when figuring the totals. For example, in the work pictured, Elizabeth made a model and wrote a multiplication algorithm for the numbers.

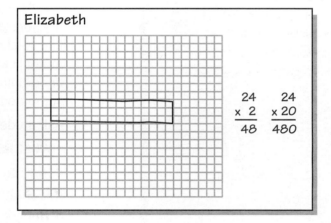

Elizabeth

$$\begin{array}{r} 24 \\ \times\ 2 \\ \hline 48 \end{array} \qquad \begin{array}{r} 24 \\ \times\ 20 \\ \hline 480 \end{array}$$

Ask questions as students share their strategies:

- **If 10 × 10 = 100, what does 20 × 20 equal?**

- **Do you multiply the 4 in 24 by 2, 20, or 24?**

Key Idea As students share and discuss their answers, point out that any number can be written as the sum of two numbers, for example:

$$24 = 20 + 4 \text{ or } 20 \times 24 = 20 \times 20 + 20 \times 4$$

Follow-Up Activity

Ask students to show the multiplication of 20 × 24 another way—as a model, patterns, an algorithm, or as the sum of two numbers.

▶ **What You Will Explore**

Students investigate multiplying numbers mentally by rounding the numbers to the greatest place. They then use basic multiplication facts and add the appropriate number of zeros.

Materials
(per student pair)
• paper and pencils

Estimate Using Mental Math

Alternate activities for **Teach** *in Lesson 12.1.*

The Task

Ask students to retell the problem using their own words.

■ **You are printing tickets for the play. Since the seats are not numbered, you need to figure out how many tickets to print. There are 26 rows of seats in the auditorium. Each row has 23 seats. How many tickets do you need to print?**

What to Look For and What to Ask

Observe students to make sure that they understand the task.

• **Do you need to know the exact number of tickets?**

• **How can you round 26 and 23 to make multiplication easier?**

• **What multiplication fact will you use?**

• **How many zeros will you add to the basic fact product and why?**

Share and Discuss

As students share their answers, discuss the strategies they used for multiplying the two rounded factors. For example, in the work pictured, Rose used a number line to show which ten is closest to 23 and 26. She then wrote down the multiplication pattern she used to multiply mentally. Rich rounded the numbers by underlining the ones digits. He used the basic fact and then counted the combined number of zeros in the factors.

Ask students questions such as:

• **What is the basic multiplication fact you used?**

• **How do you know how many zeros you will need in the product?**

Key Idea As students share their answers and strategies, point out that when multiplying by tens the product has as many zeros as there are in each factor..

Follow-Up Activity

Have students use a calculator to figure out the exact number of seats in the auditorium and then compare their estimates to the actual number. They then decide if the estimates are reasonable.

Rose

0 1 2 3 4 5 6 7 8 9 10 11 12 13 14 15 16 17 18 19 20 21 22 (23) 24 25 (26) 27 28 29 30

I first multiplied 2 x 3 = 6. I then multiplied 2 x 30 = 60,
and last I multiplied 20 x 30 = 600. That way I knew
how many zeros I needed.

Rich

2**3** rounded down is closer to 20.
2**6** rounded up is closer to 30.

20 x 30   2 x 3 = 6, so 20 x 30 = 600

2 zeros   2 zeros

Activity 13

▶ What You Will Explore

Students investigate how to estimate quotients. They use compatible numbers as well as division facts to help them in their estimation.

Materials
(per student pair)
• paper and pencils

How Close Is the Estimate?

Alternate activities for **Teach** *in Lesson 13.2.*

The Task

Ask students to pretend that they are working at a pizza place.

■ **During Saturday lunch, Pizza-By-Slice served 198 slices of pizza. If each pie has 8 slices, how many pizza pies is that?**

What to Look For and What to Ask

Observe students as they work to make sure that they have chosen an approach that will lead to a reasonable estimate.

Ask students to retell the problem in their own words.

• **Is it important to have an exact answer for this problem? Why or why not?**

• **What operation can you use to find the answer?**

• **What numbers could you use to estimate the number of pies?**

• **What do you have to remember about the groups?**

Share and Discuss

As they are working, ask students to share the numbers and operations they decided to use. For example, in the work pictured, Christina used multiplication facts and compatible numbers. Anthony used rounded numbers to estimate the number of pies.

Ask students questions such as:

• **What operation did you use?**

• **What compatible numbers did you use?**

Key Idea As students share strategies they used to estimate the number of pies, point out that when using compatible numbers you might want to use numbers that are above and below the given number.

Follow-Up Activity

Have one student use a calculator to find the exact number of pies while the other student determines if the estimates were reasonable.

Christina

$2 \times 8 = 16$,
$3 \times 8 = 24$,
$160 \div 8 = 30$,
$240 \div 8 = 30$.

They made more than 20 and less than 30 pies.

Anthony

198 is about 200,
$160 \div 8 = 20$,
$240 \div 8 = 30$,
$200 - 160 = 40$,
$40 \div 8 = 5$,
$200 \div 8 = 20 + 5$.

They made about 25 pies.

▶ **What You Will Explore**

Students investigate how to divide greater numbers. They examine different ways to use the standard division algorithm.

Materials
(per student pair)
• paper and pencils

Many Bunches of Tulips

Alternate activities for Teach in Lesson 14.1.

The Task

Tell students the following problem.

■ **The corner market has an outside flower market where they sell bunches of tulips. The wholesale flower market delivered 1,350 tulips. If there are 6 tulips in each bunch, how many bunches of tulips can be made?**

What to Look For and What to Ask

Observe students as they work to see that they are using the division algorithm in a way that will lead to a solution to the problem.

Have students retell the problem in their own words.

• **How can you find the number of bunches?**

• **If you estimate the number of bunches, about how many will you get?**

• **How does the estimate help you divide 6 into 1,350?**

Share and Discuss

As students share how they divided the tulips into bunches, discuss the strategies they used. For example, Madison used the standard algorithm. She divided each place as if it were written in an expanded notation, ending up with partial quotients. She then added the quotients. Adam used a standard algorithm, explaining each step.

You may wish to ask questions such as:

• **Were there enough thousands to divide by 6?**

• **What operations do you use when you divide using long division?**

Key Idea As students share their strategies for dividing a 4–digit number by a 1–digit number, point out that they need to place the first number in the quotient above the part of the number they are in the process of dividing.

Follow-Up Activity

Have students estimate the quotient using compatible numbers. Ask them to compare the estimates to the actual answer. Do the answers make sense?

Madison

$$
\begin{array}{r}
5 \\
20 \\
200 \\
\hline
6\overline{)1{,}350} \\
-1\,200 \\
\hline
150 \\
-120 \\
\hline
30 \\
-30 \\
\hline
\end{array}
$$

$200 + 20 + 5 = 225$

There are 225 bunches.

Adam

$$
\begin{array}{r}
225 \\
6\overline{)1{,}350} \\
-1\,2 \\
\hline
15 \\
-12 \\
\hline
30 \\
-30 \\
\hline
0
\end{array}
$$

$2 \times 6 = 12$
$13 - 12 = 1$, bring down 5
$2 \times 6 = 12$
$15 - 12 = 3$, bring down the 0
$5 \times 6 = 30$
$30 - 30 = 0$

They got 225 bunches of tulips.

What You Will Explore

Students investigate division. They use basic division facts and division patterns; related multiplication facts and multiplication patterns.

Materials
(per student pair)
- counters
- paper and pencil

Use Division Patterns

Alternate activities for Teach in Lesson 15.1.

The Task

Explain to students that in the beginning of the school year, each class receives a supply of paper.

■ **Your class received 1,800 sheets of plain paper. There are 30 students in the class. About how many sheets of paper is that for each student?**

What to Look For and What to Ask

Observe students as they work to make sure that they understand the task.

Ask students to retell the problem in their own words.

- **How can you use basic facts to divide?**
- **What if you don't know the division fact? Is there a related fact you can use?**
- **What is a multiplication pattern?**
- **What do you think a division pattern is? How can you make a division pattern?**

Share and Discuss

Ask students to share their strategies by sharing their drawings and the patterns they used. For example, in the work pictured, Charlie used a related multiplication pattern to create a division pattern to solve the problem. Jane created a division pattern by first showing the basic division fact using counters. She then created the pattern by adding zeros to the dividend and the divisor.

Ask questions as students share their strategies:

- **How are the related multiplication pattern and division pattern the same?**
- **How did you use a related multiplication pattern to help you solve the division problem?**

Key Idea As students share and discuss their answers, point out that it is important to know the basic multiplication or division facts to create a pattern in multiplication or division.

Follow-Up Activity

Ask students how many more sheets of paper each student would get, if there were only 20 students in the class.

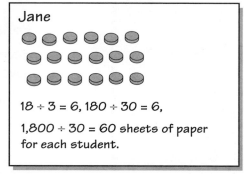

Charlie	Jane
3 x 6 = 18 3 x 60 = 180 30 x 60 = 1,800 18 ÷ 3 = 6, 180 ÷ 3 = 60, 1,800 ÷ 30 = 60 sheets of paper for each student.	18 ÷ 3 = 6, 180 ÷ 30 = 6, 1,800 ÷ 30 = 60 sheets of paper for each student.

Students investigate how to adjust the quotient to account for a remainder. They demonstrate different strategies to find the quotient.

Materials

(per student pair)
• paper and pencils

Adjust the Quotient

Alternate activities for Teach in Lesson 16.1.

The Task

Ask students to think about how they would solve the following problem.

■ **The fifth graders attend the middle school in Palisades. This year there will be 117 students going to the middle school. If each fifth grade class has 24 students, how many classes will there be? Explain your answer.**

What to Look For and What to Ask

Observe students to make sure that they understand the task. Check that they are using a strategiy that will help them to find the quotient.

Ask students to retell the problem using their own words.

• **What operation will you use to solve the problem?**

• **How can you find out how many times 24 goes into 117?**

• **Is that all you need to know?**

• **How can rounding the numbers help you?**

Share and Discuss

As students share their answers, discuss the strategies they used to find the quotient and how they used the remainder when deciding on the number of classes. For example, in the work pictured, Bonnie estimated the quotient by rounding 24 to 25 and showing that there are 4 groups of 25 in 100. She also showed that 4×24 is less than 117, while 5×24 is more than 117. She pointed out that the remainder means a fifth class is needed.

> **Bonnie**
>
> $117 \div 24$
>
> 24 is almost 25 and there are four 25s in 100 and five 25s in 125, so 4 x 24 is less than 117 and 5 x 24 is more than 117.
>
> $$\begin{array}{r} 4\ R\ 21 \\ 24\overline{)117} \\ -96 \\ \hline 21 \end{array}$$
>
> There need to be 5 classes because the 21 students need a class. So there are 4 classes with 24 students and 1 class with 21 students.

Ask students questions such as:

• **Why is it important to look at the remainder?**

• **How can you show that your answer is reasonable?**

Key Idea As students share their answers and strategies, point out that estimating the quotient provides a way to see if the answer is reasonable.

Follow-Up Activity

Have students decide how many students would be in each class if they could have only 4 classes.

▶ **What You Will Explore**

Students investigate customary units of capacity. They determine which container will provide the required number of ounces. The activity can be done with pencil and paper if measuring with water is not possible.

Materials

(per student pair)
- pint, quart, and gallon containers, labeled
- water
- paper and pencils
- Table of Measures (p. 675 of textbook)

How Many Ounces?

Alternate activities for Teach in Lesson 17.3.

The Task

Ask students to pretend that they are going to the kindergarten class to help with snack time.

- **You are going to serve the kindergarten children juice. Each child gets a 4-ounce glass of juice. There are 24 children in kindergarten. How many pint bottles, quart bottles, or gallon bottles would you need to take?**

What to Look For and What to Ask

Observe students as they work to make sure that they understand the task. Check that they work with the containers and use multiplication as needed to solve the problem.

Ask students to retell the problem in their own words.

- **How can you find out how much juice you will need?**
- **How can you find how many ounces are in each bottle?**

Share and Discuss

Ask students to share how they figured out how many ounces are in each bottle and to show their strategies for deciding how many bottles they need. For example, in the work pictured, Stephen used multiplication to find out how many ounces he needs for the kindergarten children. He then found the capacity of a pint container and used it to find the capacity of the other containers.

Ask questions as students share their strategies:

- **How many ounces in a pint?**
- **How did you decide how many bottles you needed?**

Key Idea As students share and discuss their answers, remind them that a pint is 2 cups, a quart is 2 pints, and a gallon is 4 quarts.

Follow-Up Activity

Ask students to try using a combination of bottles. How many different combinations can they discover?

Stephen

4 x 24 = 96 The Kindergarten children need 96 ounces of juice.

1 cup = 8 ounces, so 1 pint = 16 ounces.

16 x 8 = 96, so I would need 8 pints to have enough juice.

2 pints filled the quart container, and 4 quarts filled the gallon container.

So 1 gallon is the same as 4 quarts, which is the same as 8 pints.

A Milliliter or a Liter?

Alternate activities for Teach in Lesson 18.2.

The Task

Ask students to pretend that they are chefs and they are preparing soup. They are following a recipe that has the measuring units obliterated.

■ **You need to measure 3 "something" of water for the soup. Would you use liters or milliliters?**

■ **You also need 1 "something" of hot pepper sauce. Would you use liters or milliliters?**

▶ **What You Will Explore**

Students investigate metric units of capacity. They decide whether a milliliter or a liter is the appropriate unit to use.

Materials

(per student pair)

• containers with metric units of capacity written on them **or** pictures of a container holding a milliliter of liquid and a container holding a liter of liquid, with the amount written on the container

• paper and pencils

What to Look For and What to Ask

Observe students as they work to make sure that they understand the task.

Ask students to retell the problem in their own words.

• **Which is a greater unit of capacity, a liter or milliliter?**

• **Do you think you need a little water or a lot of water when you make soup? What unit would you use to measure the water?**

• **A few drops of hot pepper sauce is enough to make something very spicy. What unit would you use to measure the pepper sauce?**

Share and Discuss

Ask students to share how they figured out which metric unit to use for the water and for the pepper sauce. Encourage them to show their strategies for their decisions. For example, in the work pictured, Alyssa compared the containers by drawing pictures of each. She then wrote about her decision for her choices.

Ask questions as students share their strategies.

Alyssa

When you make soup, you use a lot of water so you need 3 liters of water.

You need very little hot pepper sauce so you use 1 milliliter.

• **Which metric unit is as big as a personal water bottle?**

• **Which metric unit measures a few drops of something?**

Key Idea As students share and discuss their answers, point out that bottles in the grocery store usually show capacity in both customary and metric units. A liter is 1,000 milliliters.

Follow-Up Activity

Ask students to write about liquids that come in bottles or containers that are about 1 liter.

▶ **What You Will Explore**

Students investigate two-dimensional figures and decide which figures are polygons and which are not. They determine the difference between open and closed figures.

Materials

(per student pair)
- drinking straws, toothpicks, or coffee stirrers
- string or yarn
- construction paper
- paper, pencils, and crayons

Make Open and Closed Figures

Alternate activities for Teach in Lesson 19.2.

The Task

Ask students to pretend they are designers.

- **You can choose to make any kind of design with yarn or straws. Fill your design with different polygons and two-dimensional figures, gluing them to sheets of construction paper. For every closed figure, make an open figure. Write the names of the closed figures inside them. What two-dimensional figures did you make?**

What to Look For and What to Ask

Ask students to explain what they are to do. Observe students' work to see that they understand the difference between closed and open.

- **How many polygons did you make?**
- **How many two-dimensional figures did you make?**
- **What are the attributes of one of your polygons?**
- **What is the name of the polygon with the greatest number of sides that you used?**

Share and Discuss

Ask students to share their designs and encourage them to show the strategies they used to create the different two-dimensional figures. For example, in the work pictured, Laura showed a house and trees made with open and closed figures.

Ask questions as students share their strategies:

- **What is a closed figure?**
- **What is an open figure?**

Key Idea As students share and discuss their designs, point out that a polygon is a closed figure with straight sides.

Follow-Up Activity

Ask students to color their designs and to name the polygon with the greatest number of sides.

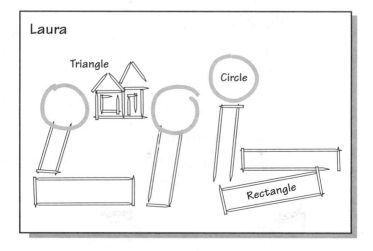

Make Congruent and Similar Figures

Alternate activities for Teach in Lesson 20.1.

▶ **What You Will Explore**

Students investigate similar and congruent figures. They create a design made with similar and congruent shapes.

Materials
(per student pair)
- dot paper
- pencils

The Task

Ask students to pretend they are designers. They can draw their designs on dot paper.

- **The city of Englewood wants a mosaic around the water fountain in the park. Only a design that is made with similar and congruent shapes will be accepted. How can you make sure your design will qualify?**

What to Look For and What to Ask

Ask students to explain what they are to do. Observe students as they work to see that they are creating both congruent and similar figures.

- **What makes figures similar?**
- **What makes figures congruent?**
- **Can figures be both similar and congruent?**
- **Can two rectangles be neither similar nor congruent?**

Share and Discuss

As students share their designs, discuss the strategies they used to determine if a figure is congruent, similar, or both. For example, in the work pictured, Felipe used congruent triangles and squares, as well as similar rectangles.

Ask the students questions such as:

- **How did you decide that your figures are congruent?**
- **How can you prove that two figures are similar?**

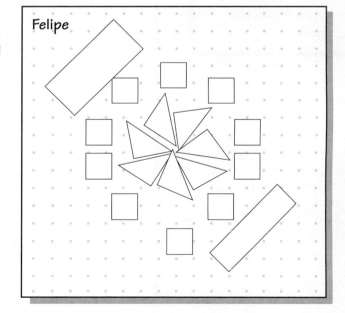
Felipe

Key Idea As students share their designs and strategies they used to determine congruence and similarity, point out that for two rectangles to be similar the relationship of the long and short sides must remain the same when the size changes.

Follow-Up Activity

Ask students to identify the congruent figures in their partner's design and to tell why the figures are congruent.

Explore Fractions of Groups

*Alternate activities for **Teach** in Lesson 21.2.*

> ### The Task
>
> Tell students the following problem.
>
> ■ There are 3 sons and 1 daughter in the Anderson family. What fraction of the family is girls? What fraction is boys?

▶ What You Will Explore

Students investigate parts of a group and show the fraction that the parts represent of the whole. They identify the numerator and the denominator.

Materials
(per student pair)
- 10 red tiles
- 10 blue tiles
- paper and pencils

What to Look For and What to Ask

Observe students as they work to make sure that they understand the task.

Ask students to retell the problem in their own words.

- **How many children are there in the family?**
- **What is a denominator?**
- **What is the numerator?**

Share and Discuss

Ask students to share their strategies. For example, in the work pictured, Bob drew a picture of the children in the family. He then represented the girl with a red tile and the boys with blue tiles. He represented the two groups with the corresponding fractions: $\frac{1}{4}$ and $\frac{3}{4}$. Daphne also used tiles, a red tile for the daughter and 3 blue tiles for the sons. She circled the individual groups to show the numerators. She then circled all the tiles to get the denominator of 4.

Ask questions as students share their strategies:

- **How can you use fractions to tell about the children in the family?**
- **What do the numerators tell about the children in the family?**

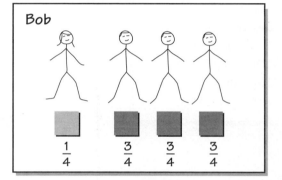

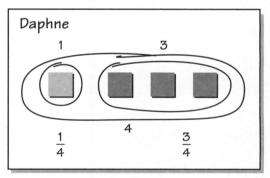

Key Idea As students share and discuss their answers, point out that the numerators add up to the denominator.

Follow-Up Activity

Ask students to use the number of boys and the number of girls in the class to write fractions. Have them also write fractions using other attributes, such as students wearing blue or white.

Activity 22

▶ What You Will Explore

Students investigate what is likely, equally likely, certain, unlikely, or impossible to happen.

Materials
(per student pair)
- 5 paper bags with tiles: bag with 4 red tiles; bag with 3 red and 1 blue tile; bag with 2 red and 2 blue tiles; bag with 3 blue and 1 red tile; bag with 4 blue tiles;
- paper and pencils

What Might Happen?

Alternate activities for Teach in Lesson 22.1.

The Task

Copy "likely," "equally likely," "certain," "unlikely," and "impossible" on the chalkboard. Tell students to follow the directions in the problem and to answer the question.

- Mrs. C is playing a game with the children in her first grade class. She wants to know which bags to use if she wants the children to pick a red tile. Examine each bag, draw the bags, and label them with what is in them and with the words on the chalkboard. From which bag are you certain you will pick a red tile?

What to Look For and What to Ask

Observe students while they work to check that they understand the problem. Make sure that they are using strategies that will enable them to solve it.

Ask students to retell the problem using their own words.

- **What does it mean for something to be "likely" to happen?**
- **When is it "impossible" for something to happen?**
- **What is the difference between something "equally likely" and "likely?"**

Share and Discuss

As students share their answers, discuss the strategies they used to determine the chances of something happening. For example, in the work pictured, Matt ordered the bags from "certain" to "impossible."

Ask students questions such as:

- **When is it impossible to draw a red tile?**
- **What does "certain" mean?**

Matt

4 red	3 red, 1 blue	2 red, 2 blue	1 red, 3 blue	4 blue
certain	likely	equally likely	unlikely	impossible

There must be some red tiles for you to pick a red tile. That's why you will certainly pick a red tile from 4 red tiles and why it is impossible to pick a red tile from 4 blue tiles.

Key Idea As students share their answers and strategies, point out that the number of red color tiles determines the outcome.

Follow-Up Activity

Have students decide from which bag they are equally likely to pick a red or a blue tile and why.

What You Will Explore

Students investigate how to add fractions with like denominators. They find how to write the sum of the added fractions in simplest form.

Materials
(per student pair)
- fraction strips
- paper and pencils

Add and Simplify Fractions

*Alternate activities for **Teach** in Lesson 23.1.*

The Task

Ask students to think about how they would solve the following problem.

- Kathy got an artist box as a gift. The box contains equal amounts of crayons, chalk, watercolor pencils, and charcoal pencils. What fraction does each art item represent? What fraction do the watercolor pencils and the crayons represent?

What to Look For and What to Ask

Observe students to make sure that they understand the task, and that they are using their fraction strips in a way that will help them to solve it.

Ask students to retell the problem in their own words.

- **How can you find out the fraction each item represents?**
- **How can you find out the fraction two items represent?**
- **How can you find the fraction that two items represent together?**
- **How can you find the simplest form of a fraction?**

Share and Discuss

As students share their fractions and additions, encourage them to show the strategies they used when simplifying the fraction. For example, in the work pictured, Sarah used fraction strips. After getting the sum of $\frac{2}{4}$, she copied the fraction strip representing $\frac{2}{4}$ and below it showed that $\frac{1}{2}$ and $\frac{2}{4}$ represented the same part of the whole.

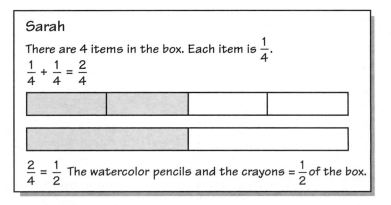

Sarah

There are 4 items in the box. Each item is $\frac{1}{4}$.

$$\frac{1}{4} + \frac{1}{4} = \frac{2}{4}$$

$\frac{2}{4} = \frac{1}{2}$ The watercolor pencils and the crayons = $\frac{1}{2}$ of the box.

Ask questions as students share their strategies:

- **How did you decide that $\frac{2}{4}$ is $\frac{1}{2}$ in its simplest form?**
- **How did you find the greatest common factor of two numbers?**

Key Idea As students share and discuss their answers, point out that all even numbers always have 2 in common.

Follow-Up Activity

Have student pairs add all the items in the box and describe the fraction they get. **Is this fraction in its simplest form? Why or why not? How can you simplify this fraction?**

Activity 24

▶ What You Will Explore

Students investigate how to subtract fractions with like denominators. They find how to write the difference of the subtracted fractions in simplest form.

Materials

(per student pair)
• fraction strips
• paper and pencils

Subtract and Simplify Fractions

*Alternate activities for **Teach** in Lesson 24.1.*

The Task

Ask students to think about how they would solve the following problem.

■ **Arvin's parents planted an herb garden. They planted basil, chives, dill, mint, oregano, parsley, sage, and thyme, one plant of each. Basil, chives, dill, and parsley are annuals. The rest of the plants are perennials. What fraction of the plants are perennials?**

What to Look For and What to Ask

Check the work students are doing to make sure that they understand the task and how to go about solving it.

Ask students to retell the problem using their own words.

• **How many plants did Arvin's parents plant?**

• **What fraction does each plant represent and why?**

• **What operation will you use to solve the problem?**

• **Can you simplify the answer? Why or why not?**

Share and Discuss

As students share their answers, discuss the strategies they used. For example, in the work pictured, Carlyle found that each plant represented $\frac{1}{8}$ of the entire garden and used fraction strips to represent the plants. He compared the answer to $\frac{1}{2}$ and concluded that $\frac{4}{8} = \frac{1}{2}$.

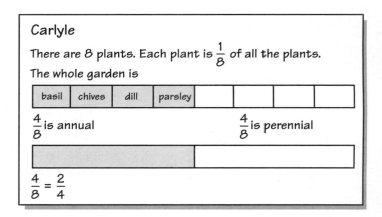

Ask students questions such as:

• **When subtracting fractions, do you subtract both the numerators and the denominators? Why or why not?**

• **Could you subtract one fraction from the other if the denominators were different? Why or why not?**

Key Idea As students share their answers and strategies, point out that they can check subtraction with fractions in the same way as they would check subtraction with whole numbers.

Follow-Up Activity

Ask students what fraction of the plants in the garden would be perennials if 6 plants were annuals?

► **What You Will Explore**

Students investigate equivalent decimals. They draw models using graph paper and use them to determine what makes decimals equivalent.

Materials
(per student pair)
- place-value chart with decimal places
- graph paper
- pencil and crayons

Make Fractions and Decimals the Same

Alternate activities for Teach in Lesson 25.2.

The Task

Tell students the following problem.

- **The kitchen floor has 100 tiles. 50 of the tiles are red. What part of the kitchen floor has red tiles? Show the part as a fraction and a decimal.**

What to Look For and What to Ask

Observe students' work with the graph paper to make sure that they understand the task.

Ask students to retell the problem in their own words.

- **How can you show the part of the kitchen floor that is red as a fraction?**
- **How can you simplify the fraction?**
- **How can you draw a model to show the decimal?**

Share and Discuss

Ask students to share how they wrote and simplified the fractions, and to show their strategies for modeling decimals and showing equivalent decimals. For example, in the work pictured, Serena wrote the fraction and simplified it by dividing by 10. She then modeled the decimal as 0.50. She showed equivalent decimals, and simplified $\frac{5}{10}$ to $\frac{1}{2}$.

Ask questions as students share their strategies:

- **What can you say about $\frac{1}{2}$ and 0.5 or 0.50?**

Key Idea As students share and discuss their answers, point out that zeros after decimal numbers do not change the decimal.

Follow-Up Activity

Tell students that of the remaining tiles 30 are yellow and 20 are black. Ask students to show these parts as decimals and fractions.

Serena

$\frac{50}{100} = \frac{5}{10}$ of the tiles are gray.

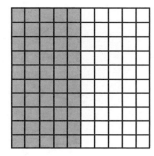

I drew a square with 10 tiles across and 10 tiles down.
I colored 50 tiles so I colored

Ones	Tenths	Hundredths
0	5	0

$0.50 = 0.5$, so $\frac{50}{100} = \frac{5}{10}$
You read the fraction and the decimal the same way.
Both are 50 hundredths or 5 tenths.
$\frac{5}{10} \div \frac{5}{5} = \frac{1}{2}$ so $\frac{5}{10} = \frac{1}{2}$

▶ **What You Will Explore**

Students investigate modeling and writing mixed numbers and decimals.

Materials

(per student pair)
- place-value chart with decimal places
- graph paper
- pencils and crayons

Model Mixed Numbers and Decimals

Alternate activities for Teach in Lesson 26.1.

The Task

Tell students the following problem.

- **Parents have volunteered to make costumes for the class play. Sally is going to be a lion. Her mom bought 2 and 75 hundredths meters of fabric. Write the length as a fraction and a decimal.**

What to Look For and What to Ask

Observe students as they work to make sure that they have developed a strategy that will help them to solve the problem.

Ask students to retell the problem using their own words.

- **How can you write the number of meters as a mixed number?**
- **In the mixed number, is the fraction part in its simplest form?**
- **How can you model the decimal?**
- **What are the equivalent mixed number and decimal?**

Share and Discuss

As students tell about the mixed number and decimal, discuss how they arrived at their answers. For example, in the work pictured, Andy used the greatest common factor when simplifying the fraction part of the mixed number. She used hundreds squares to model the decimal 2.75.

Ask students questions such as:

- **How did you write the mixed number?**
- **How can you read the decimal?**

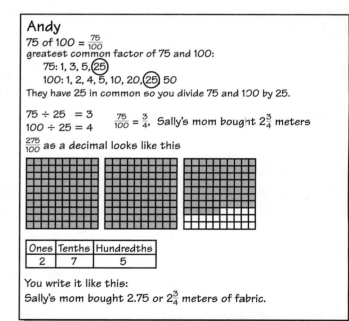

Andy
75 of $100 = \frac{75}{100}$
greatest common factor of 75 and 100:
75: 1, 3, 5, ⓐ5
100: 1, 2, 4, 5, 10, 20, ⓐ5 50
They have 25 in common so you divide 75 and 100 by 25.

$75 \div 25 = 3$ $\frac{75}{100} = \frac{3}{4}$, Sally's mom bought $2\frac{3}{4}$ meters
$100 \div 25 = 4$

$\frac{275}{100}$ as a decimal looks like this

Ones	Tenths	Hundredths
2	7	5

You write it like this:
Sally's mom bought 2.75 or $2\frac{3}{4}$ meters of fabric.

Key Idea As students share their answers, point out that in a mixed number and in a decimal you add "and" between the whole number and the fraction and between the whole number and the decimal part. The decimal part also is given its place value place.

Follow-Up Activity

Have one student of the pair model a decimal number while the other student writes the decimal and reads it.

Activity 27

▶ **What You Will Explore**

Students investigate adding decimals. They create models of the decimals and combine the models to get the sum. They use the standard addition algorithm.

Materials
(per student pair)
- graph paper
- place-value models
- paper and pencils

Use Models to Add Decimals

*Alternate activities for **Teach** in Lesson 27.2.*

The Task

Ask students to think about how they would solve the following problem.

- Mr. DeSalvo is putting up a fence on each side of his garage. He needs 2.45 yards of fencing on the left side. He needs 1.78 yards of fencing on the right side. How much fencing does he need?

What to Look For and What to Ask

Observe students' work to make sure that they understand the task.

Ask students to retell the problem in their own words.

- **How can you find out how much fencing he needs?**
- **How can you show the decimals using models?**
- **How many whole yards do you know that he needs?**
- **How can you write what you did with the models using numbers?**

Share and Discuss

Ask students to share how they modeled the decimals and to show their strategies when they added decimals. For example, students might have used grids on graph paper or place-value models to represent the decimal numbers. In the work pictured, Lisa used the addition algorithm in a place-value chart, lining up the decimal points.

Ask questions as students share their strategies:

- **How can you tell right away the least number of yards you need?**
- **Why is it important to line up the decimals?**

Key Idea As students share and discuss their answers, point out that adding with decimals is the same as adding with whole numbers. The only really important point to remember is to line up the decimals.

Follow-Up Activity

Give students other sets of decimals to add, for example 3.84 and 1.48. Ask one student to model the addition while the other student shows the addition using numbers.

Lisa

You can use numbers to find out how much fencing he needs.
2.45 + 1.78

Ones	Decimal point	Tenths	Hundredths
1	.	1	
2	.	4	5
+ 1	.	7	8
4	.	2	3

You line up the decimal point and then you add in the usual way.
So Mr. DeSalvo needs 4.23 yards of fencing.

What You Will Explore

Students investigate subtracting decimals. They create models of the decimals and they subtract one set of models from the other by x-ing out the number of squares to get the difference. They also use the standard subtraction algorithm.

Materials

(per student pair)
- graph paper
- paper and pencils

Use Models to Subtract Decimals

Alternate activities for **Teach** *in Lesson 28.2.*

The Task

Tell students the following problem.

- **Mr. DeSalvo has 5.5 yards of fencing. He used 4.23 yards of fencing to close in the yard. How much fencing does he have left?**

What to Look For and What to Ask

Observe students as they create the models to make sure that they understand the task.

Ask students to retell the problem in their own words.

- **How can you find out how much fencing he has left?**
- **How can you show the decimals using models?**
- **If you just look at the whole numbers, about how much fencing will he have left?**
- **How can you write what you did with the models using numbers?**

Share and Discuss

Ask students to share how they modeled the decimals. Encourage them to show their strategies when they subtracted decimals using the algorithm. For example, in the work pictured, Larry showed 6 grids of 100 squares to represent 5.50. He then removed the fencing that had been used by placing Xs on 4.23.

Ask questions as students share their strategies:

- **How do you show subtraction when you use models?**
- **Why is it again important to line up the decimals?**

> Larry
>
> 5.5 is the same as 5.50
>
> He used 4.23 yards. I take away 4. Then I take away 0.23. 1 and 0.27 are left so 1.27 yards of fencing is left.

Key Idea As students share and discuss their answers, point out that subtracting with decimals is the same as subtracting with whole numbers. The important thing to remember is to line up the decimals.

Follow-Up Activity

Give students other sets of decimals to subtract, for example 4.25 and 3.46. Ask one student to model the subtraction while the other student shows the subtraction using numbers.